WORLDVIEW GUIDE

HAMLET

Dr. Jayson Grieser

canonpress
Moscow, Idaho

Published by Canon Press
P.O. Box 8729, Moscow, Idaho 83843
800.488.2034 | www.canonpress.com

Jayson Grieser, *Worldview Guide for Hamlet*
Copyright ©2017 by Jayson Grieser.
Cited page numbers come from the Canon Classics edition of the play (2016),
www.canonpress.com/books/canon-classics.

Cover design by James Engerbretson
Cover illustration by Forrest Dickison
Interior design by Valerie Anne Bost and James Engerbretson

Printed in the United States of America.

A free end-of-book test and answer key are available for download at
www.canonpress.com/ClassicsQuizzes

Library of Congress Cataloging-in-Publication Data
Grieser, Jayson, author.
Hamlet worldview guide / Jayson Grieser.
Moscow, Idaho : Canon Press, [2017].
LCCN 2019011331 | ISBN 9781947644205 (paperback : alk. paper)
LCSH: Shakespeare, William, 1564-1616. Hamlet.
LCC PR2807 .G696 2017 | DDC 822.3/3--dc23
LC record available at https://lccn.loc.gov/2019011331

17 18 19 20 21 22 9 8 7 6 5 4 3

CONTENTS

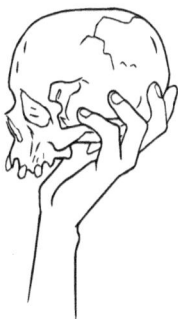

INTRODUCTION

"What's Shakespeare's greatest accomplishment?" the wise old professor asked.

"His characters," said an eager student in the front of the class, who went on to offer a list of his favorites.

"Very good. He surely did create larger-than-life characters. But actually," said the old teacher, "his greatest achievement is his language. No one ever used the English language as creatively as did Shakespeare."

The student nodded and said, "The greatest play then must be *Hamlet*, since in it Shakespeare created the roundest character who speaks the most eloquent, golden English."

"You are correct," said the professor, and rubbed his chin thoughtfully.

THE WORLD AROUND

In Shakespeare's day, during the reigns of Queen Elizabeth I (1558-1603) and King James I (1603-1625), the Bible saturated England. Erasmus had published the Greek New Testament for the first time in history in 1516. The next year, Luther kicked off the Reformation. In these two actions we have the coming together of renaissance and reformation, a renewal of scholarship leading to a renewal in Christian doctrine and life in the church.

William Shakespeare (1564-1616) imbibed the fruit of the Christian humanist scholarship in Europe: the Geneva Bible, Thomas North's popular translations of Plutarch, the essays of Michel Montaigne, William Golding's *Metamorphoses* of Ovid, and Raphael Holinshed's *Chronicles of England, Scotland, and Ireland*, to name some of his favorites.

Shakespeare published *Hamlet* around 1600, giving the world a theologically minded and wickedly eloquent student from Luther's Wittenberg. Shakespeare doesn't explain Hamlet's connection to Luther in the play, yet *Hamlet* contains all the linguistic, theological, and artistic sophistication of the age.

ABOUT THE AUTHOR

William Shakespeare probably attended grammar school in Stratford, where he would have learned Latin and studied the great Roman authors like Cicero, Virgil, Plautus, Terence, and especially Ovid. At eighteen William married Anne Hathaway, who gave him three children. Early in his career we encounter seven "lost years." When we next hear of Will, it's 1592, and he's successful enough as a dramatist to provoke fellow London playwright Robert Greene's ire for being a jack-of-all trades, "an upstart Crow," a "Shake-scene."[1]

Around 1594 Shakespeare was both actor and playwright for the elite Lord Chamberlain's Men. These same men went on to build and own the Globe Theatre (Shakespeare divided half of the ownership with five other

---

1. Quoted in *The Bedford Companion to Shakespeare: An Introduction with Documents*, ed. Russ MacDonald (Boston: Bedford/St. Martin's, 2001), 15.

actors). When James came to the throne in 1603, the new king took this premiere troupe into his patronage, renaming them the King's Men. As a playwright, Shakespeare devoted a decade mostly to comedies and histories before turning to tragedies, including the four greats—*Hamlet*, *Othello*, *King Lear*, and *Macbeth*—and finally, at the end of his career, to tragic-comedies such as *The Winter's Tale* and *The Tempest*.

WHAT OTHER NOTABLES SAID

Though Shakespeare lacked the university-level classical education of his contemporary Ben Jonson (also a playwright), Jonson finds Shakespeare a greater poet than the ancients:

> And though thou hadst small Latin and less Greek,
> [...]
> Leave thee alone for the comparison
> Of all that insolent Greece or haughty Rome
> Sent forth [...].[2]

Even though Shakespeare did not have a university education (hence the comment about small Latin and less Greek), Jonson lauds him as a man "not of an age but for all time!" He is the "Sweet Swan of Avon!" and the

2. Ben Jonson, *To the Memory of My Beloved the Author, Mr. William Shakespeare and What He Hath Left Us.*

"Soul of the age! / The applause, delight, the wonder of our stage!"[3]

England's first poet laureate, John Dryden, also picks up on Shakespeare's outdoing of the ancients and his natural (not university) learning:

> [Shakespeare] was the man who of all modern and perhaps ancient poets had the largest and most comprehensive soul.... When he describes anything, you more than see it, you feel it too. Those who accuse him to have wanted learning, give him the greater commendation: he was naturally learned; he needed not the spectacles of books to read nature; he looked inwards, and found her there.[4]

In *L'Allegro,* John Milton continues to praise Shakespeare's "natural" genius. Shakespeare is "Fancy's child," who "warbles his native wood-notes wild." In the twentieth century, T.S. Eliot similarly says, "We can say of Shakespeare, that never has a man turned so little knowledge to such great account."[5]

---

3. *To the Memory of My Beloved the Author, Mr. William Shakespeare.*

4. *Essay of Dramatic Poesy* (London: Henry Herringman, 1668).

5. T.S. Eliot, *To Criticize the Critic and Other Writings* (Lincoln, NE: University of Nebraska Press, 1965), 148.

SETTING, CHARACTERS AND PLOT SUMMARY

- *Setting:* Denmark at some imprecise time in the 13th or 14th century.
- *The Ghost:* Purports to be the former King of Denmark and Father of the Prince, Hamlet
- *Hamlet:* Son of the late (Old) Hamlet, King of Denmark, and Queen Gertrude
- *Queen Gertrude:* Hamlet's mother, Old Hamlet's widow, now married to King Claudius
- *King Claudius:* Brother of Old Hamlet, and recently elected King of Denmark
- *Horatio:* Close friend to Hamlet, student
- *Polonius:* Courtier at King Claudius's court
- *Ophelia:* Daughter of Polonius
- *Laertes:* Son of Polonius, brother of Ophelia

- *Rosencrantz and Guildenstern:* Old friends of
  Hamlet's, brought from England to the court of
  Elsinore (the castle) by King Claudius
- *Fortinbras:* Son of the dead (old) Fortinbras,
  leader of the army of Norway in his father's
  absence

Questions and fears open the play. Soldiers on the bat-
tlements whisper that the Ghost may appear again! The
skeptical student Horatio doubts the apparition, claiming it is nothing but a thing of fantasy. But he too sees
the Ghost in the image of their former king and proposes
taking the news to Prince Hamlet. While King Claudius
speaks to the court of his marriage to his brother's widow,
Hamlet stands aloof, in black, in grief. He speaks his **first
soliloquy** ("O that this too, too solid flesh would melt,"
1.2.133-164).[6] Horatio then tells him of the Ghost, and
Hamlet decides to join the next night's watch. At their
meeting, the Ghost, claiming to be his murdered father,
calls for revenge. In his **second soliloquy** ("O all you hosts
of heaven!" 1.5.99-119), Hamlet vows to wipe clean his
mind of all except the words of the Ghost. Hamlet makes
his friends swear secrecy and speaks of himself putting on
an "antic disposition" (1.5.192).

Ophelia, a young lady at the court who has repelled
Hamlet and his love letters, enters the stage frightened

6. All line numbers refer to the Folger Shakespeare Library edition of
Hamlet, ed. Barbara A. Mowat and Paul Werstine (New York: Simon
& Schuster, 2012).

by Hamlet's apparent madness. Her father, Polonius, identifies Hamlet's behavior as "the very ecstasy of love" (2.1.114) and decides to put Ophelia in Hamlet's way to see if his love for her can dispel his madness. Hamlet's old friends, Rosencrantz and Guildenstern, also try to endear themselves to Hamlet, but Hamlet knows they are pawns of Claudius.

A troop of actors arrives, and Hamlet requests they perform "The Murder of Gonzago," a play in which a king is murdered by his nephew—with some added lines of Hamlet's own. In his **third soliloquy** ("O what a rogue and peasant slave am I," 2.2.576-634), Hamlet berates himself for his inaction. He will observe his uncle at the play to confirm the word of the Ghost, for fear it may be a devil trying to damn him.

Rosencrantz and Guildenstern fail: they have no explanation for Hamlet's strange ways. Claudius will see "Hamlet's" play, but agrees to test Polonius's suspicions first by spying on Hamlet and Ophelia. Hamlet speaks his **fourth soliloquy** ("To be or not to be," 3.1.64-96), and then berates Ophelia with some very harsh and vulgar language. Ophelia laments Hamlet's losing his "noble mind."

Hamlet directs the players, telling them to "hold up a mirror to nature" to make the performance as lifelike and unexaggerated as possible (3.2.23-4); he directs Horatio to watch his uncle. In the play, as the nephew poisons his uncle Gonzago's ears, Claudius rises and exits the hall.

Hamlet and Horatio agree that it was "the talk of poisoning" that stung the king (3.2.315).

Hamlet agrees to visit his mother but first speaks his **fifth soliloquy** ('Tis now the very witching time of night," 3.2.419-432). King Claudius soliloquizes about his sin and finally kneels to pray. Hamlet enters, draws his sword, but on second thought, fears sending him to heaven (here he speaks his **sixth soliloquy**, "now might I do it pat," 3.3.77-101). As Hamlet confronts his mother, she calls for help. Polonius is spying on them and cries out, and Hamlet stabs him through the curtain, thinking he is Claudius. As Hamlet castigates his mother for marrying Claudius, the Ghost reappears to Hamlet. At this point, Hamlet sees himself as heaven's "scourge and minister" (3.4.196).

Claudius, needing to protect himself, sends Hamlet to England with a request to the King of England to execute Hamlet on arrival. On his way, Hamlet crosses paths with Fortinbras, a soldier on his way to fight for a worthless piece of land. Hamlet, in his **seventh soliloquy** ("How all occasions do inform against me," 4.4.34-69), confesses he doesn't know why he has not killed his uncle. His thoughts will now "be bloody or be nothing worth!"

As a result of her father's death at the hands of Hamlet, Ophelia goes insane with grief and starts singing mad songs; Polonius's son, Laertes, returns from France with a mob and threats. Claudius appeases Laertes by telling him that Hamlet has been captured by pirates and is returning to Denmark. Claudius plans a deadly fencing match between Laertes (with a poisoned rapier) and Hamlet; Claudius also says that he will offer Hamlet a poisoned cup, just in case Laertes cannot wound Hamlet with the poisoned rapier. Before this, however, news comes that Ophelia has drowned, further incensing Laertes against Hamlet.

Hamlet returns to Denmark, and at a graveyard, he and Horatio meditate on death as Ophelia's funeral procession enters. Laertes and Hamlet are so grief-stricken that they both leap into her grave and grapple with one another.

In the last scene, Hamlet tells Horatio that on his way to England he discovered the king's death sentence hidden in the baggage of Rosencrantz and Guildenstern. Hamlet switched their letters with a forgery of his own, damning Rosencrantz and Guildenstern to death. Despite knowing the king's duplicity, Hamlet accepts the duel and apologizes to Laertes. In the match, Hamlet does well and Claudius offers him the poisoned cup. Hamlet refuses, but his mother drinks instead. During the duel, Laertes hits Hamlet with the poisoned foil, and in the confusion that follows, Hamlet strikes Laertes with the poisoned foil.

When the Queen dies, Laertes accuses the king of treachery, and Hamlet stabs Claudius with the foil and forces him to drink from the cup, killing him. Laertes and Hamlet exchange forgiveness before dying. Hamlet prevents Horatio's suicide; he must tell Hamlet's story. As Fortinbras arrives, Hamlet gives his consent for Fortinbras to ascend the Danish throne.

WORLDVIEW ANALYSIS

"To be or not to be—that is the question" is no doubt the most famous line in *Hamlet,* and probably in the world. And it reminds us that the play is a play of questions. The play's first line is a question; the play is suffused with questions. These questions are more significant than we might think. One of the greatest literary minds of the twentieth century put it this way:

> There's no other play in Shakespeare, which probably means no other play in the world that raises so many questions of the 'problem' type. It's quite clear that problems, genuine or phony, *are a part of the texture of the play, and central to its meaning.* I'm not saying we get the 'real meaning' of the play by figuring out answers to its problems: I'm saying quite the opposite. Insoluble problems and unanswerable questions meet us everywhere we turn, and make *Hamlet* the most stifling and claustrophobic of plays. Not for

us, because we're outside it, but for the characters
caught up in its action.[7]

If the questions are "unanswerable," why read the play?
We do so because great literature requires interpretation.
A great work of art like *Hamlet* is subtle; it leaves room
for the imagination. As Noah Lukeman notes, the subtle
writer "will often leave things unsaid, may even employ a
bit of confusion, and often allow you to come to your own
conclusions."[8] We the readers (or viewers) have to, in a
sense, finish the story.

The thorniest problems of the play, the same problems
readers of *Hamlet* have always wrestled with, include: Is
Hamlet mad? Does Gertrude know of Claudius's fratri-
cide? Is the Ghost really Hamlet's father? Should Hamlet
act now on the Ghost's word or delay? All the fun is in
forming our own readings of particular lines and scenes
and then sharpening our own interpretative blade on the
opinions of others, whether professional productions of
the play, scholarly articles, or our classmate's argument
across the table from us.

---

7. Northrop Frye, *Northrop Frye on Shakespeare* (New Haven, CT: Yale
University Press), 84; emphasis added.

8. *The First Five Pages: A Writer's Guide to Staying Out of the Rejection
Pile* (Oxford: OUP, 2010), 159.

The Ghost

As we've seen, Hamlet himself lives in a stifling, claus-trophobic world, a world he calls an "unweeded garden" (1.2.139). And if that isn't bad enough, *Enter Ghost.* When Hamlet sees the Ghost, he sees (or thinks he sees) his Father, and he's so unhinged he fails to discriminate between good and evil:

> Be thou a spirit of health or goblin damned,
> Bring with thee airs from heaven or blasts from hell,
> Be thy intents wicked or charitable,
> Thou com'st in such a questionable shape
> That I will speak to thee. I'll call thee "Hamlet,"
> "King," "Father," "Royal Dane." (1.4.44-50)

Hamlet's worldview includes Heaven and Hell and a ghost. Is the Ghost real? Even the skeptical young scholar Horatio thinks so. And Horatio, like Hamlet, thinks he can identify the apparition: the Ghost, he says, is "our last king" (1.1.92), "the King your father" (1.2.197, 199). This "father" claims to be from Purgatory, and claims to reveal the truth to Hamlet, refuting King Claudius's spin:

> Now, Hamlet, hear.
> *'Tis given out that,* sleeping in my orchard,
> A serpent stung me. So the whole ear of Denmark
> Is by a forgèd process [a false story][9] of my death
> Rankly abused [grossly deceived]. But know, noble youth,
> The serpent that did sting thy father's life

9. Any glosses in brackets I've taken from the Folger Shakespeare Library's edition of *Hamlet*.

Now wears his crown. (1.5.41-47, emphasis added).

Hamlet responds as if he suspected avuncular treachery: "O, my prophetic soul! My uncle!" (48). If we go back to the second scene of Act 1, we see Hamlet nauseated by his mother's and uncle's hasty marriage, and the speed with which the whole court "moved on." For Hamlet, who remained in black, something was awry! Hamlet's intuitions were correct.

Claudius's lie about the death of Old Hamlet (that he was stung by a serpent) reveals an important truth: a serpent did sting the king. Marjorie Garber speaks of Claudius as a "satanic" figure driven by lust for power, stinging the good king at rest. She calls this "Eden myth" in the garden "the play's riddle, the center of its radiating imaginative energy...its primal scene."[10] When Caroline Spurgeon speaks of the problem that infects Denmark, she speaks of it "as a *condition* for which the individual himself is apparently not responsible, any more than a sick man is to blame for the infection which strikes him down and devours him...."[11] Claudius is the offending Adam who sins in the garden; Hamlet is the son who inherits the false king's cursed world. Shakespeare conveys Denmark's sick condition with images of "sickness, disease

---

10. Marjorie Garber, *Shakespeare After All* (New York: Anchor, 2005), 489.

11. Caroline Spurgeon, *Shakespeare's Imagery and What It Tells Us* (New York: The Macmillan Company, 1936), 319; emphasis in original.

or blemishes of the body."[12] We see this in Hamlet's first soliloquy:

> O God, God
> How weary, stale, flat, and unprofitable
> Seem to me all the uses of this world!
> Fie on't, ah fie! 'Tis an unweeded garden
> That grows to seed. Things rank and gross in nature
> Possess it merely. (1.2.136-141)

What can Hamlet do to weed this "rank and gross" "un-weeded garden"? He ends his meeting with the Ghost reluctant but duty-bound: "The time is out of joint. O cursèd spite / That ever I was born to set it right!" (1.5.210-11). But being a believer in Heaven and Hell, Hamlet's weeding of this garden must give him pause. Can he be sure of the Ghost's word? Can he, as a Christian, pursue revenge? If he dies trying, will he go to some purgatorial realm like his father, or maybe someplace worse?

Hamlet's Delay

His "Father" tells him: "But, howsomever thou pursues this act, / Taint not thy mind, nor let thy soul contrive / Against thy mother aught. Leave her to heaven…" (1.5.91-93). Even with this moral guidance—which lends some credence to the Ghost really being his father—Hamlet is a reluctant avenger. While Hamlet believes it is his fate to avenge his father, he demands confirmation of the Ghost's

---

12. Spurgeon, *Shakespeare's Imagery*, 316.

summons. Though Hamlet claims that he will "sweep to [his] revenge" (1.5.37), he's actually more successful with his antic acting than with any action against Claudius. By the opening of the Second Act, two months have elapsed. He's done nothing. Why?

One answer is—he doesn't know himself. It's a mystery. Hamlet chastises Guildenstern for attempting to "pluck out the heart of my mystery" (3.2.395-96).[13] But let's try to discover (remember our part as interpreters?) Hamlet's motivations. To probe deeper, let's turn to the play's most celebrated soliloquy, the first part of the "To be or not to be" speech.

> To be or not to be—that is the question:
> Whether 'tis nobler in the mind to suffer
> The slings and arrows of outrageous fortune,
> Or to take arms against a sea of troubles
> And, by opposing, end them. To die, to sleep—
> No more—and by a sleep to say we end
> The heartache and the thousand natural shocks
> That flesh is heir to—'tis a consummation
> Devoutly to be wished. (3.1.64-72)

"To be or not to be—that is the question." Is *what* "to be or not to be"? Is Hamlet referring to suicide? Maybe. But let's consider the next line. Which is "nobler in mind"? Is it nobler "to suffer / ... or to take arms against

---

13. See also the seventh soliloquy in which Hamlet says he doesn't know why he hasn't taken action (4.4.46-49).

a sea of troubles"?[14] To suffer would be easier than to act. Why? Because if Hamlet takes action against "a sea of troubles," he may die. And what comes then? The conclusion to the soliloquy refers again to action or the lack of action in general. Given the context, this meditation hints at Hamlet's thoughts of killing Claudius.

> Thus *conscience* does make cowards of us all
> And thus the native hue of resolution
> Is sicklied o'er with the pale cast of thought,
> And enterprises of great pitch and moment
> With this regard [on this account] their currents turn awry
> *And lose the name of action.* (91-96, emphasis mine)

"Conscience" can be defined as "internal reflection, inner voice, inmost thought."[15] Thought of what? What comes after death. Hamlet's belief or "dread" about what comes after death might seem odd. Why is his view of the afterlife so bleak? This soliloquy reveals Hamlet's state of mind within the poisoned world of the play. As we've seen, Hamlet is a hero for whom such an act as killing the king is freighted with eternal significance. What can he do now? As Hamlet puts it, "the play's the thing wherein

---

14. The note in the back of the Folger Shakespeare Library's *Hamlet* sees this as a scholarly debate—the kind of thing Hamlet would take up at Wittenberg—a philosophical question: "Which is the nobler action, suicide or acceptance of a painful life?" (291). But there's perennial debate about the meaning of this soliloquy.

15. David and Ben Crystal, *Shakespeare's Words* (London: Penguin Books, 2004), s.v. "Conscience," http://www.shakespeareswords.com/Headwords-Instance.aspx?Ref=2716 (accessed June 10, 2017).

I'll catch the conscience of the King" (2.2.633-34). At the play, Hamlet will "hold ... a mirror up to nature" (3.2.23-24)—he will attempt to expose the king's conscience and assuage his own. (Hamlet will even insert some of his own lines into the play.) The play-test works. Claudius visibly reacts to the poisoning (in Hamlet's play Luciano *the nephew* poisons the bad king!). Even the skeptical scholar Horatio accepts the proof; he too sees Claudius rise in response to the ear-poisoning in the Mousetrap play.

> Hamlet: "O good Horatio, I'll take the ghost's word for a thousand pound. Didst perceive?"
> Horatio: "Very well, my lord." (3.2.312-13)

Hamlet heeds the biblical admonition to "test the spirits" (1 Jn. 4:1); and having confirmed the truthfulness of the claim, he's ready to shed blood.

His opportune moment comes. Hamlet finds the king alone and defenseless, on his knees mumbling towards heaven. Hamlet enters, draws his sword, and says to himself, "Now might I do it pat [opportunely], now he's a-praying, / And now I'll do't" (3.3.77-78). But he pauses. Another thought enters his mind—"And so he goes to heaven [...]"? (79). Is sending Claudius to Heaven revenge? No. Hamlet will wait...he'll wait to catch his uncle in sin, so he can damn him. This desire for his uncle's damnation, says Sister Miriam Joseph, is Hamlet's fatal flaw: he has forsaken justice and "tainted his mind" with "personal hatred."[16]

In a five-act Renaissance tragedy, the climax or crisis, the turning point that allows no turning back, usually comes in Act 3. Once the die is cast, complications mount, leading inevitably to the catastrophe. Hamlet has made his decision not to kill the serpent-king when he had the chance; then he kills Polonius, thinking him to be the king. The king hears and sends Hamlet to England. Ophelia, the one Hamlet claims to love, goes mad as a result of Hamlet's murder of her father. Laertes returns and demands justice. The king sets up the match: Laertes will face Hamlet to the death, a match the king will poison just as he has poisoned the kingdom.

Death & Providence

As the play moves into the fifth act, Hamlet faces death. He meditates on death with Horatio at the graveyard. He reflects on the deaths of Yorick and Alexander and "Imperious Caesar" (5.1.190-91; 216-221). He learns of Ophelia's death. But he also begins to reveal a faith in providence. He speaks of "a divinity that shapes our ends, / Rough-hew them how we will" (5.2.11-12). He speaks of "heaven" as "ordinant" in the execution of Rosencrantz and Guildenstern (5.2.54). He will fight against the odds in a match against Laertes, trusting, he says—alluding to

16. Sister Miriam Joseph, "Hamlet: A Christian Tragedy," *Studies in Philology* 59, no. 2, part 1 (April 1962): 131.

the Gospel of Matthew—that "there is a special providence in the fall of a sparrow" (5.2.233-34). In this final
act, Hamlet's dark but Christian worldview brightens, if
only a little.

In the catastrophe, Hamlet is poisoned, Laertes is poisoned, Gertrude is poisoned—and Hamlet now, after the
long delay, kills the poisoner, assured of the justice of his
action. He chokes the serpent on his own venom; he slays
him with his own poisoned sword. Clear victory, right?
Yet the tone of the ending is complex. As Oscar Mendel
puts it, "Tragedy concerns a hero on whom we are to be-
stow our good will; but it need not concern a hero who
really *excites* our sympathy."[17] Our response to Hamlet's
end may be mixed: he's simultaneously one we *fear* (that
is, we don't want to be in his shoes) and one we *pity*.[18] As
another scholar puts it, Hamlet's end is simultaneously a
failure and a victory.[19] He purges the kingdom of Denmark and secures the forgiveness of Laertes and the eulo-
gy of Horatio, but he couldn't prevent the catastrophe or
the loss of the kingdom to Fortinbras.

---

17. Oscar Mendel, *A Definition of Tragedy* (New York: New York
University Press, 1961), 89.

18. Aristotle claims that tragedy produces a catharsis involving fear and
pity. See his definition in *Poetics*, 1449b.

19. Pat Rodgers, ed., *Oxford Illustrated History of English Literature*
(Oxford: Oxford University Press, 1987), 138.

So What?

So what? Why should this play matter for us today? Turgenev thought Hamlet a picture of most modern people, an egoist and a skeptic, a man with faith in nothing. Hamlet "does not know what he is after, nor why he lives at all, and still [he] firmly adheres to life."[20] Roy Battenhouse believes Hamlet to be anything but an exemplary Christian; rather Hamlet is a narcissist whose revenge quest is pagan and thus hopelessly misguided.[21] I grant that what these critics say is worth pondering, but I think they have missed the heart of Hamlet.

While a flawed man, Hamlet is no skeptic. To call the world an "unweeded garden" is to profess a higher ideal; it is to know what the world *should* be.[22] Consider this: though a nihilist might think it his right to take his own life rather than face the abyss of brokenness and loss, Hamlet believes in the "Everlasting [God]" (1.2.135) who has condemned suicide. A law exists outside of himself, a law he must *obey*. Nor does Hamlet believe—like so many moderns—that everyone who is "true to himself" automatically dies a blissful death. He is mortified that he may *do the wrong thing* and be damned for it.

---

20. Ivan Turgenev, "Quixote and Hamlet," *Chicago Review* 17, no. 4 (1965): 95-96.

21. Roy Battenhouse, *Shakespearean Tragedy: Its Art and Its Christian Premises* (Bloomington: Indiana University Press, 1969), 231, 238-240.

22. G.K. Chesterton, "The Orthodoxy of Hamlet," in Dorothy Collins, ed., *Chesterton on Shakespeare* (London: Cox and Wyman, n.d.), 60-61.

The traditional tragic hero, say, Oedipus or Antigone, demands the truth even if it destroys him or her. Hamlet is similar, but more *thoughtful* of the consequences. He spends his time philosophizing, playing with words, playing a role, avoiding the enterprise of "great pitch and moment." He prefers the safer world of thought, but he knows that he must eventually go on to *do* something big. But Hamlet will act only with a clean conscience. After berating himself for thinking too hard, for not living up to his ideal, the ideal of a son who risks all to vindicate his father, in the end he acts with a clean conscience and faith in a "*special* providence," that is, a providence that rules over every detail of his life.

Hamlet holds a mirror up to our lives, for we too must act in a fallen world, even when the way is unclear and when our proof is dismissed by others. We too are called to kill serpents, to "lose all" for the kingdom. Because it takes great courage to confront the enemy and might cost us our reputation or our lives, we, like Hamlet, would rather think and play with words than act. And like Hamlet's, our lives will be remembered as a mixture of success and failure. We'll have gotten things wrong; we'll have acted rashly or too late. Friends and foes will read our obituaries quite differently. One may call us a God-fearing person, another "a silly believer in an antiquated book."

Much in this play and in this man eludes us, just as much in ourselves and in the world eludes us. In the character Hamlet, whether or not we are fully conscious of it, we behold a reflection of ourselves, more accurately and mysteriously than in any other work of literature. That's what makes this the most celebrated play in the world.

QUOTABLES

1. "O, that this too, too sullied flesh would melt,
   Thaw, and resolve itself into a dew,
   Or that the Everlasting had not fixed
   His canon 'gainst self-slaughter! O God, God,
   How weary, stale, flat and unprofitable
   Seem to me all the uses of this world!"

   ~Hamlet, 1.2.133-38

2. "Something is rotten in the state of Denmark."

   ~Marcellus, 1.5.100

3. "There are more things in heaven and earth, Horatio,
   Than are dreamt of in your philosophy."

   ~Hamlet, 1.5.187-188

4. "Though this be madness, yet there is method in't."

   ~Polonius, 2.2.223-24

5. "What a piece of work is man, how noble in reason,
    how infinite in faculties, in form and moving how
    express and admirable; in action how like an angel, in
    apprehension how like a god: the beauty of the world,
    the paragon of animals—and yet, to me, what is this
    quintessence of dust?"

    ~ Hamlet, 2.2.327-332

6. "The play's the thing
    Wherein I'll catch the conscience of the King."

    ~ Hamlet, 2.2.633-34

7. "To be or not to be—that is the question:
    Whether 'tis nobler in the mind to suffer
    The slings and arrows of outrageous fortune,
    Or to take arms against a sea of troubles
    And, by opposing, end them."

    ~ Hamlet, 3.1.64-68

8. "Get thee to a nunnery. Why wouldst thou be
    a breeder of sinners?"

    ~ Hamlet, 3.1.131-32

9. "The lady doth protest too much, methinks."

    ~ Queen Gertrude, 3.2.254

10. "Now cracks a noble heart. Good night, sweet prince,
    And flights of angels sing thee to thy rest."

    ~ Horatio, 5.2.397-99

21 SIGNIFICANT QUESTIONS AND ANSWERS

1. What are foils in *Hamlet* that can help us interpret the play?

    When you think of a foil, think of tinfoil under a diamond. A character who is acting as a foil is one who by contrast shines light on another. In this play, full of questions, we can look to the foils in the play—Laertes, Fortinbras, and Ophelia—to get some traction interpreting the play's protagonist. In terms of character and action, we can contrast Laertes and Fortinbras with Hamlet (all of whom have lost a father). We can also contrast Ophelia's madness with Hamlet's. As we do so, we find that, generally speaking, Laertes and Fortinbras act rashly while Hamlet is delayed and thoughtful. (Laertes says he'll cut Hamlet's throat in the church, for example, and Fortinbras is going off to war for a strip of Poland.) In both cases, these men of action are

contrasted to the man paralyzed by his conscience.
Another foil is Ophelia: her madness is clinical
whereas Hamlet's is, at least mostly, "put on."

2.   Is the Ghost to be trusted?

This is perhaps the most important question, one
every reader must consider, and a great question for
students to debate. Hamlet has three options: the
Ghost is of his imagination, of the devil, or of God.[23]
Since others corroborate the reality of the ghost,
the first is eliminated. Hamlet at first assumes the
Ghost to be his father and submits to his wishes (Act
1). By the end of Act 2, he isn't so sure. He fears in
his "melancholy" he may be deceived by the devil.
Thus he takes up the play-within-the play to test the
Ghost's word. Only after he and Horatio both see
the King's seemingly guilty response does Hamlet re-
gain confidence in the Ghost's identity and trustwor-
thiness.[24] Is Hamlet correct about the identity of the
Ghost? He has his own intuition, his "own prophetic
soul," and the play which held a mirror up to his uncle's deed and provoked him to rise. Horatio sees this
too. But the Ghost's identity is never *absolutely* clear.

---

23. For a good discussion of this triad, see Sister Miriam Joseph's
"Discerning the Ghost in Hamlet," *Publications of the Modern Language
Association of America* (1961): 493-502.

24. "Discerning the Ghost in Hamlet," 497. For a different view, see
Peter J. Leithart, *Brightest Heaven of Invention* (Moscow, ID: Canon
Press, 1995), 117-162.

3. How does Horatio's worldview differ from Hamlet's?

> The famous line: "There more things in heaven
> and earth, Horatio / than are dreamt of in your
> philosophy" (1.187-88) suggests that Horatio's
> assumptions about the world differ from Hamlet's.
> Horatio's initial skepticism about the Ghost makes
> him a valuable check against Hamlet's passionate
> and wild supernaturalism. If the skeptical and stoic
> Horatio can be convinced, that's saying something.
> We should note too that Horatio is Hamlet's friend
> who sticks with Hamlet to the end, so while they
> differ, they do share a lot in common.

4. What of Polonius? Is he a buffoon?

> A good place to look for answers would be his
> long-winded instructions to his son, Laertes.
> We should notice he speaks in platitudes. In his
> officiousness, he even sends a spy after Laertes.
> He's the one who famously says, "This above all: to
> thine own self be true…." (1.3.84). While this bit
> of tripe is often attributed to Shakespeare himself,
> Shakespeare didn't say this: Polonius did.

5. What of Claudius's character?

> Claudius comes across as politically shrewd (he's
> not a buffoon like Polonius, who is his chief court-
> ier). The new king wisely recognizes the danger
> of Fortinbras taking advantage of a weakened

Denmark during his transition (he claims this fear justifies his hasty marriage). He speaks tenderly, if pompously, to his nephew, Hamlet, trying to solace his grief. He also remarks at times of his own bruised conscience. Though Shakespeare complicates his character in these ways, overall he plays the role of the Machiavellian (a man who only cares about his political power).

6. Since we see him at prayer, why can't we say Claudius repents?

He doesn't actually pray; he talks about prayer. Nor does he repent. He wants to keep his crown, ambition, and queen (3.3.59), though he recognizes that's not possible, if he truly repents. In the prayer scene, Shakespeare gives him some great lines, including "Bow stubborn knees, and heart with strings of steel / Be soft as sinews of the newborn babe" (3.3.74-75). Since he doesn't repent, it is difficult to feel sympathy for him, although some readers do—the scene is that dramatically powerful.

7. What of Gertrude? What does she know?

She tells Hamlet: "O Hamlet, speak no more! Thou turn'st my eyes into my very soul, / and there I see such black and grained spots / As will not leave their tinct" (3.4.99-102). What is she guilty of exactly? Adultery? Complicity in the murder? Both?

8. Is Ophelia best thought of as a victim?

> Ophelia is a victim in that her father is murdered
> and this leads to her madness, if we can take her
> mad songs in act 4 as truthful (they seem to be).
> Hamlet victimized her by sleeping with her before
> marriage (again if we can trust her song) and then
> by carelessly killing her father. But we shouldn't
> see her as simply a doormat. She's smart. She's
> the one who says, "O, what a noble mind is here
> o'erthrown!" She recognizes Hamlet as the "rose
> of the fair state" and chastises herself for sucking
> "the honey of his musicked vows" (3.1.163-170).
> In sum, she's both a sympathetic character, but she
> also has a mind of her own.

9. Should Hamlet kill Claudius when he finds the king
   alone at prayer? Is this moment the climax of the play?

> Roy Battenhouse thinks Hamlet should have tried
> to care for Claudius, instead of buying into his
> "father's perspective."[25] But if Hamlet is the avenger
> who must cleanse the kingdom of its poisoner, then
> he should kill the serpent. After the confirmation of
> the play-test he finds the king alone and draws his
> sword. But then he decides he must not only kill,
> but also secure his uncle's damnation. He assumes
> Claudius to be in prayer and thus repentant. This
> is a chilling moment. In the next scene, Hamlet
> rashly stabs through the curtain and kills Polonius.

25. *Shakespeare's Christian Dimension* (Bloomington, IN: Indiana University Press, 1994), 383.

Once he has shed blood he can no longer hide from the king; thus there's no turning back. To find the climax we must reason back from the catastrophe (the final disaster) and ask what action put this conclusion into motion. These two errors of Hamlet's seem to be key. Either the failure to kill Claudius or the killing of Polonius, since it introduces Laertes as avenger, may be thought of as the climatic moment.

10. Is revenge wrong in Hamlet's context?

Queen Elizabeth I and James I both forbade private revenge. However, most people in Shakespeare's day sympathized with a son avenging a father seeing it as a "dreadful but sacred duty."[26] Hamlet obviously wrestles with this question: he imagines himself the one called to set things right (1.5.210-12). Later in the play he calls himself a "scourge and minister" (3.4.196). He must not pursue revenge privately or out of personal hatred. It seems he must wait for the divinely appointed time to seek public justice.[27]

11. Are the obstacles to Hamlet's revenge internal or external?

The conflict is one between his moral conscience and duty to his "father." What Shakespeare does is take the typical revenge story and complicate it

---

26. Seymour Kleinberg, *The Reader's Encyclopedia of Shakespeare*, s.v. "Revenge."

27. Fredson Bowers, "Hamlet as Minister and Scourge" *PMLA* 70, no. 4 (1955): 747.

and transform it into a story of self-discovery. In other words, the obstacles seem mostly related to conscience. External factors may be: what evidence does he have that would hold up publicly? Should he charge in and confront the King as Laertes does? Hamlet wisely chooses to confront the king indirectly with the play.

12. Rosencrantz and Guildenstern arrive to spy on Hamlet; Polonius and Claudius will spy on Hamlet and Ophelia. Who else is spying in the play? Why?

In the David Tennant movie version of Hamlet, security cameras constantly focus in on anyone in the castle. Everything is under surveillance. Why? Trust has broken down; everyone is spying on everyone else and everyone is playing a part. Acting (pun intended by Shakespeare) becomes a major theme of the play.

13. Why is Hamlet interested in the players' speaking of "Priam's slaughter"?

Priam is the King of Troy, so his murder matches up with Demark's own situation. One interesting study is to look for all the ancient hero references in the play. Old Hamlet fought a duel against old Fortinbras. Hamlet chastises himself for not being like his father but knows that somehow he can't. His intellect and eloquence and conscience occupy him for most of the play rather than fighting like an action hero. He must suffer into truth.

14. Hamlet turns out to be a bad man, no? He has blood on his hands and could have prevented all of the deaths, in fact. How do we not condemn him?

> The tragic hero is always a flawed man. But he must also be or have been a good man. If he's an evil man from the start, his death would be deserved and not tragic. Ophelia speaks of Hamlet's character: "O, what a noble mind is here o'erthrown!" (3.1.163). Hamlet's attempt to purge the kingdom of its snake is not like Macbeth's. In this play, Claudius would be the Macbeth character. The Ghost initiates the revenge, and Hamlet tests the Ghost. Hamlet goes on to entangle himself in the sin of the kingdom, to be sure; and thus his ending is a mixture of success and failure. However, I don't think we ever lose our admiration for him, nor our horror at his mistakes. He's both attractive and repulsive.

> On the puzzling nature of Hamlet, G.K. Chesterton writes, "the more flatly irreconcilable are the opinions of various men about Hamlet, the more he resembles a real man." And "Hamlet was not fitted for this world; but Shakespeare does not dare to say whether he was too good or too bad for it."[28]

15. The Gravedigger scene is such a change of tone. What is Shakespeare doing in this scene?

---

28. "The True Hamlet," in *Chesterton on Shakespeare*, 41, 43.

Hamlet, in this poignant scene, perhaps the greatest of all scenes, speaks to skulls and meditates on death. "Adam" is mentioned by the gravedigger, giving this a universal application.[29] We will all die. Hamlet accepts death and comes forth from the grave a new man, a humbled man, one with trust in God.

16. Hamlet speaks of a "special providence in the fall of a sparrow." Is this a change in his outlook?

It seems to be, though some see Hamlet as a fatalist (rather than a man of faith) when he says "the readiness is all" (5.2.236-37). But his belief is in a special providence as opposed to fate or even a general providence. And of course the sparrow comes from Matthew's Gospel. His new readiness for action might be flowing out of the King's attempt to send him to England to be executed, Ophelia's death, and his time in the graveyard smelling skulls and philosophizing.

17. Why all the soliloquies?

Henry V is a man of action who can make a great speech on the battlefield, but doesn't soliloquize, except in a prayer right before battle. By contrast, Hamlet is a man of stunning language and wit, rather than action, which the soliloquies showcase. In the soliloquies he shares his mind with us.

---

29. Maynard Mack, "The World of Hamlet," *Yale Review* 41, no. 502 (1952): 59.

18. What was the original story of Hamlet?

> The old Norse folk tale of Amleth provided
> Shakespeare with most of the characters. A Dane
> named Saxo Grammaticus recorded the story in
> Latin around 1200 AD and then a French writer
> named Belleforest elaborated on the story. The
> original lacks all the complications Shakespeare
> added to it. No ghost. The killer's identity is never
> in question. Amleth never delays or doubts. After
> he burns down the courthouse and kill his uncle,
> he proclaims himself king.[30]

19. Horatio will live to tell his story. What does this mean?
    What kind of story is it?

> So shall you hear
> Of carnal, bloody, and unnatural acts,
> Of accidental judgments, casual slaughters,
> Of deaths put on by cunning and forced cause,
> And, in this upshot, purposes mistook
> Fall'n on th' inventors heads. All this can I
> Truly deliver. (5.2.422-428)

> Most of this I think is describing Claudius, though
> "accidental judgments, casual slaughters" probably
> applies to Hamlet. A good passage to debate with
> students.

---

30. Michael Dobson, and Stanley Wells, ed., *Oxford Companion to Shakespeare*, s.v. "Hamlet, Prince of Denmark," 180.

20. What does it mean that the play is a tragedy?

A dramatic tragedy will involve a fall from happiness to misery or even death. Usually early in the play a hero of high degree makes a tragic choice which leads him to a crisis or climax. At this point the story unravels, leading inevitably to a catastrophe in which the disorder in the city is purged and order is restored. A tragic hero is blind to certain things, and this blindness produces powerful ironies. But he is also extreme, even superhuman, in his tenacity for his ideals, pushing against anyone or anything that might deny him.

21. Does Hamlet finally act in good conscience?

Late in the play Hamlet tells Horatio that now, according to his conscience, he must act against Claudius: "Is it not with perfect conscience / to quit him with this arm? And is 't not be damned / to let this caner of our nature come to further evil? (5.2.75-80). Hamlet seems to have come full circle on this question. He now must act against Claudius. And when he does kill him he is acting as a public avenger of his father's poisoning. Bowers calls Hamlet's action against the king an "open killing [...] a ministerial act of public justice accomplished under the only possible circumstances." Hamlet has purged the kingdom but not without getting tangled up in its fallenness.[31]

---

31. Bowers, "Scourge and Minister," 749.

FURTHER DISCUSSION
AND REVIEW

Master what you have read by reviewing and integrating the different elements of this classic.

SETTING AND CHARACTERS
Be able to compare and contrast the personalities (including strengths, weaknesses, and mannerisms) of each character. Which characters change over the course of the play? Which do not?

PLOT
Be able to describe the beginning, middle, and end of the play along with specific details that move the plot forward and make it compelling.

CONFLICT
Go through the character list and describe the tension between any and all main characters. Then, think about

whether any characters have internal conflict (in their own minds). Is there any overt conflict (fighting), or conflict with impersonal forces?

THEME STATEMENTS

Be able to describe what this classic is telling us about the world. Is the message true? What truth can we take from the plot, characters, conflict, and themes (even if the author didn't believe that truth)? Do any objects take on added meaning because of repetition or their place in the story (i.e., do any objects become symbols)? How does the author use perspective, tone, and irony to tell the truth?

- Human beings are unfathomable creatures made in the image of God, and we cannot ever "pluck out the heart of [their] mystery."
- We are not born into an Eden, but into an "unweeded garden," and like Hamlet we not only deal with our own sins, but with the results of a world ruined by sin in which we often face difficult moral dilemmas.
- We are called to contemplate and meditate on the consequences of our actions, even if we can rarely foresee them.

A NOTE FROM THE PUBLISHER:
TAKING THE CLASSICS QUIZ

Once you have finished the worldview guide, you can prepare for the end-of-book test. Each test will consist of a short-answer section on the book itself and the author, a short-answer section on plot and the narrative, and a long-answer essay section on worldview, conflict, and themes.

Each quiz, along with other helps, can be downloaded for free at www.canonpress.com/ClassicsQuizzes. If you have any questions about the quiz or its answers or the Worldview Guides in general, you can contact Canon Press at service@canonpress.com or 208.892.8074.

ABOUT THE AUTHOR

Dr. Jayson Grieser has a PhD in literature from the University of Dallas after completing a dissertation on the poetry and perspectives of George Herbert. He teaches at New Saint Andrews College in Moscow, Idaho. He and his wife Hannah have five sons.